MILNER CRAFT SERIES

Paper Tole
THREE DIMENSIONAL
DÉCOUPAGE

Paper tole on cover by Anne Plowman from
Oz -Can Paper Craft, Perth.

First published in 1992 by
Sally Milner Publishing Pty Ltd
558 Darling Street
Rozelle NSW 2039 Australia

Reprinted 1993 (twice)
Revised edition 1994

© Judy Newman 1992

Photography by Andrew Elton and André Martin
Printed in Slovenia

National Library of Australia Cataloguing-in-Publication data:

Newman, Judy.
Paper tole

ISBN 1 86351 144 X

1. Paper work. 2. Découpage. 3. Handcraft. I. Title. (Series:
Milner craft series).

745.546

Contents

Introduction

In recent years many paper crafts have been revived — découpage, papermaking, papier maché and marbling are among these creative techniques. All were practised centuries ago — the methods are old — but, with our modern materials and printing methods, and a fresh eye to design, the results are certainly new.

Among these techniques has surfaced paper tole, an offshoot of découpage and probably the least known of all the paper crafts. Most people, on looking at a paper tole work for the first time, are mystified. It looks so complex, and difficult. The lack of printed information on the technique has added to this sense of mystery.

This book explains paper tole techniques from the simplest level, including step-by-step pictures, and gives many illustrated examples of diverse projects, which will teach even beginners the basics of this fascinating craft. Once the basic techniques are mastered, it takes only practice and patience to complete even the most complicated paper tole picture. You can then use the range of beautiful wrapping papers, greeting cards and prints available to us today to create original works.

Most paper tole artists like to frame their work, but paper tole is equally suited to making wall hangings, cards, box tops, Christmas decorations and other works for your home. Enjoy and discover the possibilities presented by this, as yet, largely unexplored craft field.

WHAT IS PAPER TOLE?

The art of paper tole is also known as three-dimensional découpage, and indeed it is an exciting expansion of découpage techniques. It involves cutting out sections of identical prints and layering them with silicone glue between each layer to create a three-dimensional picture.

The cut-out paper pieces are gently shaped and curved or positioned at an angle to give realism to the picture, and each layer is carefully built up to give a third dimension to particular sections of the picture. The completed work is often varnished to protect it and to blend the layers together visually while emphasising certain areas of the design.

HISTORY OF PAPER TOLE

Little is known about the history of paper tole. The word 'tole' is thought to have come from the French word describing the craft of beating metalware into a raised shape to give it pattern.

Paper tole is thought to be an extension of découpage and probably appeared in Europe after découpage became popular in the eighteenth century. One form of découpage, known as *Vue d'Optique*, or shadow boxes, involves elevating areas of a picture using papier maché or cardboard to hold up the area to be raised. Sometimes multiple prints are used for this, and this seems to be the forerunner of paper tole techniques. Works of *Vue d'Optique* were usually mounted under glass in a shadow box.

Découpage thrived throughout the Victorian era, but during this time it was more a form of collage than découpage. The designs were busy, pretty and feminine, with overlapping images that covered the entire surface of the object. Several other paper crafts popular in the Victorian era — including scrapbooks, Valentines and greeting cards stitched on perforated paper — found their way into découpage. Boxes, tea trays and screens were often covered with Valentines, scrapbook pictures and cards.

Today many people have rediscovered the beauty of découpage and other paper crafts. It is not surprising that paper tole — one of the most fascinating of the paper crafts — has re-emerged.

Acknowledgements

The author and publisher wish to thank the following paper tole artists for their contributions to this book:

- Kathryn Elsworth, paper tole artist, who was consulted in the production of this book and completed some of the projects in it. Kathryn began paper tole by completing an Anton Pieck work, a complicated piece which still stands as one of her favourite pieces. She is also fond of Brambly Hedge scenes and those from Foxwood Tales.
- Anne Plowman, who worked the 'Fairy Princess' and 'In the Gazebo'. Anne has been practising paper tole for many years and has been a leader in popularising the craft in Western Australia. Anne's company, Oz-Can Paper Crafts, Perth, produces a paper tole range that includes early Australian scenes, wildlife and wild flowers.
- Lyn Cunningham, who worked the 'Columbine Flower Fairy' and the 'Sweetpea Blossom Baby' pictures. Lyn's company, Paper Tole Creations, Melbourne, produces prints for paper tole featuring May Gibbs illustrations, the Flower Fairy series by Cicely Mary Barker and the Brambly Hedge illustrations.

The author and the publisher also wish to thank Andrew Elton and André Martin who photographed the works in this book.

The following individuals and organisations have kindly given their permission for the following materials to be reproduced in this book:

- Solocraft Ltd, West Yorkshire (material from a kit of prints of 'The Toy Shop' by Anton Pieck).
- Carol Wilson Fine Arts, Inc., Oregon ('Carol's Rose Garden' greeting card by Celene Ryan).
- Oz-Can Paper Crafts, who print 'The Fairy Princess' and 'In the Gazebo' and others in the same series.
- Paper Tole Creations, who print 'Sweetpea Blossom Baby' and 'Columbine Flower Fairy' and others in the same series.

These works are copyright and should not be reproduced for commercial purposes.

Prints from greeting cards, wrapping paper, calendars, diaries and books can all be used for paper tole.

Chapter 1

Materials and Equipment

Very little equipment is needed for this craft, making it easy to start and inexpensive to continue. Once you have a suitable print (in multiple copies), you really only need cutting equipment, glue (silicone sealer) and varnish. Some people also like to use tweezers to handle the small cut-out pieces of paper. Accessories such as a self-healing cutting mat and tools for shaping the paper pieces may be useful, but they are not essential.

PRINTS FOR PAPER TOLE

Sources

Prints from greeting cards, wrapping paper, calendars, diaries and books can all be used for paper tole. Six to eight prints of the same picture are usually needed, but four or five will suffice for simpler pieces.

Many paper tole artists purchase six or eight copies of beautifully illustrated books, which yield a source of many prints and may actually work out cheaper than individual greeting cards.

The weight of the paper will affect cutting. It is best not to use thick paper and cardboard as they are more difficult to cut.

Suitable images

Regardless of the source of prints, the main concern is the image itself.

Probably the most important concept for beginners to understand is the choice of prints that are suitable for paper tole. With experience, you will be able to judge whether a print will work well, but initially, look for the following two things in your prints.

1. Clear outlines

Choose pictures which have a clear outline around the images. Those with a definite outline around each image or colour area are much easier to cut than those with images that have blurred edges (such as watercolour wash areas which are not clearly defined) or dotty brushstrokes (such as those in many oil paintings), which will be impossible to cut around clearly. A clear line around images in the picture not only makes cutting easier, but it also enhances the effect of layering.

The Brambly Hedge illustrations by Jill Barklem are a good example of delightful pictures which have clear outlines. *The Flower Fairies* series of books by Cicely Barker are also excellent for paper tole.

Look at the examples we have used in our projects and you will eventually become used to looking for pictures containing images with clear outlines. Once you start your paper tole work, you will realise the importance of these outlines — they are *so* much easier to cut out.

2. Background and foreground

In order to build dimension in your paper tole picture, there must be definite background and foreground parts to the scene. The best effects in paper tole are gained by using pictures with these clear background and foreground areas, which can be built up by layering middleground over background, then foreground over middleground sections, giving the effect of dimension.

In our scene by artist Stephen Bevan, 'The Fairy Princess' (see p. 23), the bluebell flowers are set in the background, the mouse, the fairy and the tree roots in the middle ground and the mushrooms, flowers and leaves in the foreground. The mushrooms, flowers and leaves have been accentuated even more by being raised and extend out in front of the framing mat, which has been cut smaller than the picture.

The look of a picture can be varied by the amount of detail worked and by the extent to which certain areas of the design are raised. However, to achieve a realistic effect and correct dimension, you must always work within the framework of the background, middleground and foreground.

Beginners should avoid pictures with too much detail. Eventually, with experience, you will be able to tackle more adventurous projects, but, at first, you may be overwhelmed if you take on a large and very detailed picture, such as one of the larger Anton Pieck scenes popular with paper tole artists (see 'The Toy Shop' on p. 15 in our section on '*Basic Techniques*'). Prints depicting very detailed scenes such as vases of flowers are also quite difficult for a beginner, as there will be many very fine details to cut out and handle.

CUTTING EQUIPMENT

Once you have chosen your prints, much of the work is in cutting out. Use either surgical scissors, a craft knife or an artist's scalpel to achieve clean edges and precise cuts. Whichever cutting instrument you choose, make sure it is sharp. Always cut with the knife, or scissors, on the right-hand side of the area you are cutting (if you are right handed), enabling you to see the piece clearly and to cut accurately.

Scissors

Surgical scissors are handy for cutting curves. Always remember to move the paper through the scissors rather than the scissors around the paper — this way you will achieve a more even line. Remember also that the scissors must be sharp. A clean edge is needed — not a ragged edge which you will be left with if you use blunt scissors. Some people prefer to cut roughly around the shape with scissors then trim the piece with a scalpel or craft knife. It is best, however, to make your cut as cleanly as possible the first time so that you don't waste sections of your prints.

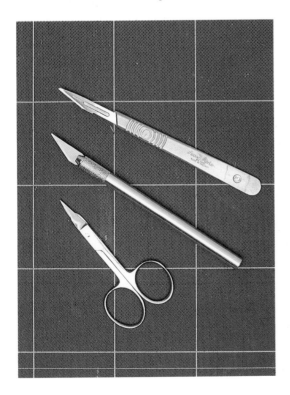

Surgical scissors, a craft knife or an artist's scalpel will give clean edges and precise cuts.

Craft knife or artist's scalpel

Use either a craft knife or an artist's scalpel for cutting out. Artist's scalpel (available from graphic design suppliers and art supply shops) usually has a finer blade and therefore gives a slightly better result. However, many people find a craft knife is just as effective. Either knife, fitted with a sharp blade, is essential for cutting detailed areas and small angled sections of your prints.

Cutting mat

Self-healing cutting mats are used by graphic artists and patchworkers because they provide a non-slip surface for cutting, saving tabletops from scars. The use of a cutting mat is optional. Many people simply cut out their print on a wad of newspaper or a magazine.

GLUES

Silicone sealer (clear-drying) is used to layer the cut-out pieces on top of each other. A dab of glue is applied to the background print (not the cut-out piece), and the cut-out piece is then superimposed over the top of the print. The glue holds the cut-out pieces in place and elevates them at different levels to give dimension to the picture.

Silicone sealer is chosen because it holds its shape and doesn't run or shrink on drying. Clear-drying Window and Glass Sealant by Dow Corning is suitable. Check the labels for safety warnings and follow the manufacturer's advice.

VARNISH

Most paper tole artists like to varnish their finished picture to highlight areas and to blend the various layers. Some also recommend sealing the back of the prints before cutting in order to strengthen the prints for fine cutting and to prevent oil staining from the silicone adhesive.
The varnish must be designed for use on paper. Liquitex Gloss Medium and Varnish or Liquitex High Gloss Varnish are suitable.

Apply the first coat of gloss very thinly and allow it to dry. Add two thick coats, without excess brushing, leaving each coat to dry before applying the next. Use a quality brush.

TWEEZERS

You may like to use tweezers to hold tiny cut-out paper pieces, and to manoeuvre pieces into the desired position.

COCKTAIL STICK OR MANICURE STICK

This tool is perfect for manoeuvring the tiny cut-out pieces of paper into position when they are placed on top of the silicone. The pointed end is perfect for angling the paper pieces and for pressing gently in just the right spot to achieve the desired shape. It is also handy for applying a tiny smear of silicone to thin paper pieces or for touching a dab of silicone to a cut-out button or bow tie which is too small for handling with fingers.

TOOLS FOR SHAPING

Shaping the cut-out pieces of your picture is essential to give a realistic effect. A plastic shaping tool and a soft mat are now available. Use the tool to sculpt the paper pieces — space flower petals, curve the sails of a boat or fill out the skirt on a dress. Resting the paper piece on the mat will support it while it is being shaped.

FELT PENS AND SOFT LEAD PENCILS

When the paper pieces are cut out, they will often have a white cut edge. If left, it will detract from your work, so it should be shaded to blend with the rest of the picture. Do this by running a felt pen or soft lead pencil along the cut edge. Choose the same colour as the area to be cut out. Test your paper first, as some pieces may be very absorbent, soaking up too much colour from the felt pen. In that case use a pencil.

Detail from *The Flower Fairy* series
(see opposite page).

The delightful scene in this paper tole picture is from *The Flower Fairy* series by artist Cicely Mary Barker. It was worked by Lyn Cunningham.

Chapter 2

Basic Techniques

ASSESSING THE DESIGN

The first step is to decide which area of the picture to highlight — that is, which area will be built up and brought forward above the rest, and which areas you will allow to recede into the background.

There should be three main levels in your finished picture — the background, the middleground and the foreground. Decide which areas of the picture you want to fall into these levels of perspective. Remember to be guided by logic — if you are working on a picture of a shop window, the items in the front of the window should be more 'raised' than those at the back. Figures of people in front of the window will obviously be more raised than anything in the window.

Generally a good guideline to follow is to work from the back to the front of the picture. If your scenes feature people, deal with the background, then the figures in the picture, then 'dress them'. Often the most raised part of a figure will be the face, an arm in front, a hat or a bow tie.

Flowers in a vase will deserve to be highlighted by being brought forward more than the vase. And the stamens will probably be raised more than the petals because they are usually 'on top'.

Some pictures will have parts which need to be placed behind the background to make them recede in the distance. To do this the piece is cut out from one print, with an allowance, a tab or 'seam' around it. It is then glued behind the starting print, from which that section has been removed. (For details see the section on 'Overcutting' on p. 10.)

Decide, vaguely anyway, how your picture should be layered. Now you are ready to start cutting.

Cutting is the step which will determine the finished effect, and it is this step that will develop your skill with practice. Your sense of perspective will develop with experience, giving your paper tole pieces a better dimension. Two paper tole artists given the same picture will want to highlight different areas — so it is also a matter of individual choice.

CUTTING OUT

Once you have decided which sections of the design to highlight, it is time to start cutting. You usually need at least six of the same prints to achieve enough different levels in your picture. If you don't have quite enough, one or two colour photocopies can be used in the middle sections.

To begin, leave one print completely intact; this will be the background to your picture. Then, working from back to front and remembering how you have decided to layer your picture, cut out each layer of the picture. Cut exactly along the outline of each piece. You may want to go on to the next step and layer some parts before cutting out the rest. This will enable you to see how the work is progressing.

These instructions will make much more sense when you've had a little experience. Choose a set of inexpensive prints to practise on! Wrapping paper with a repeat design is probably the cheapest source of prints. On a more expensive project, you can practise layering the pieces as you cut, before you glue them in place.

Some helpful tips

- Cut exactly on the outline of each image.
- For the pieces which you will be building up, cut away any background that may show through in the centre of the image.
- Cut cleanly, without torn corners or ragged edges.
- Always be aware of safety — keep your fingers clear of the direction of the knife.
- Try to cut a bevelled edge on your paper to avoid a white line showing on the cut edge. Do this by angling the blade so that the surface is slightly larger than the underside.
- You'll find cutting easier if you pull the knife towards your body rather than away from you. That way you'll have more control of the knife because you'll be guiding it from your shoulder rather than your wrist.
- Keep the knife on the right-hand side of the piece you are cutting to enable you to see it clearly (if you are right handed). Reverse this procedure if you are left handed.

- Cut conservatively, without chopping into other areas of your print. You may need the other sections later.
- You will need extra pieces of the parts you want to build up. So, you will need only one, two or three cut-outs of middle and background sections, but for the foreground items you will need five or six cut-out pieces. These pieces will not all have the same amount of detail. After all, you want layers of different levels, not just six of the same areas cut out and placed on top of one another. For example, if you are layering a figure, cut out the whole figure and then, say, her jacket. Then, from another print, cut out the most prominent arm. Also cut out extra pockets and buttons or other details. If there is a frill on the jacket, you can cut it out, to add after the other details.

CUTTING WITH TABS

In order to raise prominent areas of a design, some pieces need to be cut with tabs. When positioning the cut-out piece, the tab is inserted through a slit in the background or the piece underneath. The tab can't be seen but it supports the cut-out piece, giving it height.

To cut a tab, cut out the piece in the usual way, but add an extra area — that is, the tab — where the piece will meet the background, usually at the base. For example, in the 'Fairy Princess' picture on the cover, the stalks of the mushrooms were cut with a tab. A slit was then made in the background print and the tab of the mushroom stalk was inserted. Thus, the stalk is raised at a sharp angle, because it is supported by the tab. The tree roots were worked in the same way.

This technique also works well with flower petals, leaves or wherever you want a piece to angle sharply out of the background.

OVERCUTTING
Making parts of your background recede

If you want a small part of your background to recede behind the rest of the background, say the scene outside an open door, this can be achieved by cutting it out and placing it behind the starting print.

Using a spare print, cut out the parts to be receded. Leave an allowance (which is also called a seam or a tab) around the piece so that there is no edge visible in the area which will be behind the starting print. Then, take your starting print — the one with the background and foreground intact — and cut out, exactly on the line, the sections to be receded (this time with no seam).

Glue the pieces with the seam (from the spare print) to the back of the starting print, aligning them exactly and with dabs of silicone around the cut-out section of the starting print. Adjust the cut-out piece to line up with the main print.

SHAPING, CURVING AND ANGLING CUT-OUT PIECES

After pieces are cut out and before you glue them on in layers, they should be shaped to give realism to the picture. Shape each piece around your fingers or use a shaping tool and flip the edges slightly so they curve towards the back of the print, making the cut edges less conspicuous.

Be guided by the natural shape of each object. A sail on a boat can be gently curved to billow out from the mast; a flag or a horse's tail can ripple gently with the wind; ears on a rabbit may flop forward slightly; walls of a house should be angled appropriately, and so on. Once you have placed the pieces on the background print, on top of the silicone glue, use the cocktail stick to lift up corners or to angle a piece in a certain direction. In the project 'Fairy Princess', for example, the toadstool

A shaping tool and a soft mat will enable you to sculpt and shape the paper pieces.

caps in the foreground have been shaped into realistic curves, flower petals are curved up and the dress and hair appear to ripple and drape. Use a pad of felt, or a specially designed soft mat, and shaping tools (see 'Tools for Shaping' on p 5) to help you sculpt the cut-out paper pieces in a realistic manner.

FEATHERING

Fur, feathers and hair will be difficult to cut out because of the ragged edges. The best way to deal with these images is to use a sharp knife or a pair of scissors to cut zigzag edges with fine points, which will look more real than if you cut around the shape in a curve.

LAYERING

Once the pieces are cut and shaped, you can begin to build your picture. Work on the cutting mat or a sheet of cardboard. Apply the silicone gently, in spots 2–3 mm high, to the background print rather than to the piece to be applied. Keep glue in the centre of the area, away from cut edges — you don't want it visible in the finished picture or squashing out from under the edges. Avoid getting glue on your fingers — this would make handling cut-out pieces difficult. Place the cut-out piece onto the silicone spot, and then use the cocktail stick to angle the piece as desired.

Continue building the layers, shaping and angling pieces as you go. For very tiny cut-outs, apply a thin smear of silicone to the centre of the area using the point of the cocktail stick.

The glue takes several minutes to dry, so you will have plenty of time to adjust the position of each piece.

As you work on higher levels, don't press on built-up layers. If the glue isn't dry, those beneath might be compressed. Also, don't touch the layers with the nozzle of the glue tube — it might push the layers down.

Each level of the picture should be at least a few millimetres ($\frac{1}{10}$") higher than the previous one. Vary the height depending on the amount of dimension you wish to achieve. Don't allow more than about 3 mm ($\frac{1}{8}$") between each level, as too much of a gap will become evident when the picture is viewed from an angle.

As you work, hold up the picture to eye level every so often, and check that the layers are level. Often when you are working on a flat tabletop, you will be inclined to position the top layers slightly too low. When your

Build up layers of paper tole with glue, shaping and angling the cut-out pieces as you work.

finished piece is framed it will be viewed at eye level; if layers aren't correctly positioned, this may spoil the finished effect.

VARNISHING

When your picture is complete, varnish can be used to highlight the foreground or other areas as desired. This is optional, but in some cases it does serve to blend the levels of the picture more fluidly, giving a smoother sense of dimension. Some paper tole artists like to varnish their pieces to give them the appearance of a porcelain plaque.

Use a watercolour varnish, or sealer which dries clear and smooth. Apply it with a soft brush and use two or three coats, depending on the finish you desire. You might like to apply one coat to the whole picture and then additional coats to the top layers. For some pieces, you may decide not to use varnish at all.

MOUNTING AND FRAMING

If you wish to frame your work, a shadow box frame or a frame with a spacer bar is needed to accommodate the depth of the picture. Glass will protect the piece from dust.

Professional framing is recommended. However, this can become quite expensive and there are a number of other suitable applications for your paper tole work. You can mount paper tole on a painted wooden hanger to make a delightful and inexpensive gift. Boxes, especially those with a recessed lid which are designed to be fitted with embroidery, can be used to hold a paper tole work. Christmas decorations can be mounted on heavy cardboard, and trimmed with ribbon. Refrigerator magnets, mobiles and even lampshades can all be decorated with paper tole.

This charming Anton Pieck scene, *'The Toy Shop'*, was worked by Kathryn Elsworth using prints from a kit by Solocraft Ltd. It is more suitable for experienced paper tole artists. Note the complex layering involved in the shop window to give a true perspective to the many separate items featured. The pieces have also been carefully shaped after cutting, which adds to the depth of the picture. The picture has been varnished and is now ready for mounting and framing.

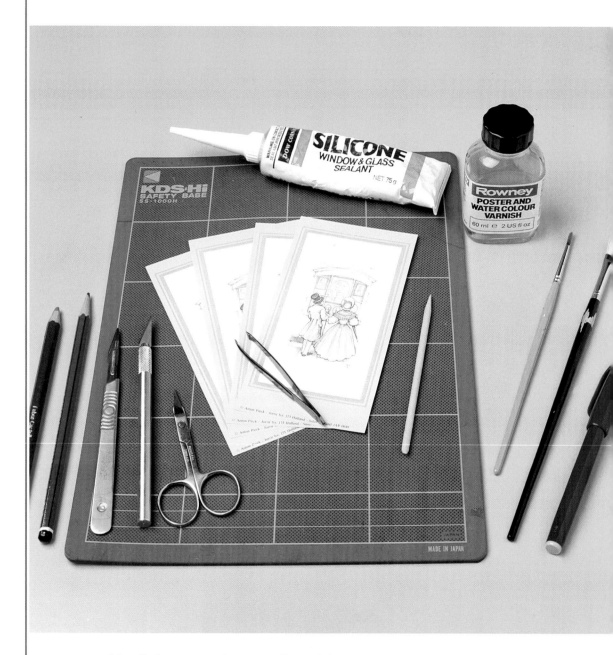

Assemble all the materials you will need for a paper tole project before you begin. Note that Liquitex Gloss Medium and Varnish or Liquitex High Gloss can also be used as a varnish.

Chapter 3

Projects

BEFORE YOU BEGIN

- Before you attempt any projects, read the 'Basic Techniques' chapter of this book and assemble all general materials required.
- You will usually need a minimum of six (and possibly eight) identical prints for each paper tole picture. For simpler renditions, four or five prints will suffice.
- Of course, you won't always be able to work on a project using exactly the prints illustrated in this book, so for other pictures, choose the most similar style of print — that is, if you want to work a floral project, see our 'Box with Pansies' (p. 33) or 'Rose Wall Hanging' (p. 41).
- Cut out your pieces for paper tole carefully, following the tips given in Chapter 2 on 'Basic Techniques'.
- As you assemble your work, remember to shade in any cut edges with a felt pen.

GENERAL MATERIALS FOR ALL PROJECTS

- Set of six to eight identical prints of the same image (four or five for simpler pieces).
- Sharp surgical scissors.
- Artist's scalpel or sharp craft knife.
- Cutting mat.
- Clear-drying silicone sealer.
- Clear-drying (water colour) varnish.
- Soft brush, to apply varnish.
- Tweezers (optional).
- Cocktail or manicure stick.

IN THE GAZEBO

This tranquil scene by artist Stephen Bevan was worked by Anne Plowman. Its simplicity and clearly outlined figures make this small project perfect for those who are not experienced in paper tole techniques. Note the built-up areas such as the fountain, woman's clothing and the railing, and the cleverly slanted seat, all of which give the picture a realistic perspective.

STEPS

1.   The house will be slightly raised from the background print. To do this, cut a slit in the background print at the base of the house. From a second print, cut out the house (including the woman's head), together with a tab on the base. Insert the tab into the slit, aligning the bushes in front of the house.

Stephen Bevan – Oz Can

"IN THE G/

2.   After you have cut out the greenery pieces, there will be many white edges remaining as a result of the fine cutting that is required around the fronds. To ensure that the greenery blends into the rest of the picture, it is important to colour the white edges with a green marking pen. Ensure that all the edges are thoroughly covered.

Instructions

1. For the purposes of this paper tole project, 'In the Gazebo' can be divided into three areas. In the background is the house and the garden, the middleground includes the gazebo with the woman and the cat, and the foreground contains the water fountain. One print will remain as the base upon which the rest of the picture will be constructed. On this base print, cut a slit around the bushes so the bottom edge of the house can be fitted in behind them. From the second print, cut out the house, cutting around the entire house and including the bushes. Slip the cut out piece into the slit in the base print until the bushes on both the base print and the second print align. See Step 1.

2. From a third print, cut out the chimney, including a tab at the base. Shape the chimney piece (see p.11), creating an edge along its corner. On the base print, make a slit at the bottom of the chimney and insert through it the tab of the chimney just cut out from the third print. Also from the third print, cut out the bay window, the roof and the front verandah and glue them in place.

3. The ferns. Do the ferns next, working a couple of layers for the best effect. Cut the fronds carefully along the dark outlines. Colour the cut edges with a green marker and then gently curve the fronds using a shaping tool and mat. Carefully glue the ferns in place.

4. The gazebo. Cut out the gazebo in one piece, paying particular attention to shaping and curving the iron roof, the posts and the railing. Cut extra pieces for the seat, and angle the seat base out from the floor when gluing it in place.

5. The woman. Cut out the woman in one piece but without her feet. Add the feet separately and then, on top of these, add an extra layer of shoes. Carefully layer and shape the dress to give it dimension and to make the folds on it look real. Cut out extra collar pieces and glue them in place. Also, cut out the arms separately, and bend them forward when you position them in place. For best effect, it is advisable to also cut the hands separately, with a tab at the end of each wrist, which should then be inserted into the bottom edge of each sleeve. Cut a separate book and fix it in the woman's hands. Finish the woman by cutting out an extra head piece including only the right-hand side of her hair.

6. The Cat. Work the cat by cutting it out twice. Shape the cat so that it is quite rounded at the edges before you glue it in place. Add an

extra head, which should also be shaped and slightly tilted when it is fixed in position.

7. The water fountain. The fountain is positioned in the foreground, and is therefore worked last. First, cut the fountain out whole with a tab at the base. Insert this tab into the bottom line of the base print. Shape the fountain out from the base of the print in a concave direction, and then cut out the whole rim of the top. Shape the back of the rim in a concave direction and the front in a convex direction. Glue the back of the rim to the last print, allowing the front to project forward. Cut out one spout piece and fix it in place. Carefully cut out an extra ball on top of the spout and glue it in position.

8. Cut out the decorative trim under the bowl, shape the piece with the appropriate edges and angles, and then carefully glue it in place. This step completes the construction of 'In the Gazebo'.

9. Varnishing. To finish this paper tole picture, varnish it as you wish, to give it the effect that you particularly desire. In the illustrated example, all the raised parts of the picture have been given a glossy finish with a coat of varnish.

10. Framing. The finished picture was mounted and framed professionally. A double mat was included around the picture to give it extra dimension.

THE FAIRY PRINCESS

Fantasy scenes are fun to do in paper tole and they make delightful pictures to hang in a child's room. 'The Fairy Princess' is a picture painted by artist Stephen Bevan. This paper tole project was worked by Anne Plowman.

STEPS

1.   The bluebells in the background are carefully shaped using a shaping tool and soft mat. Cut out the entire flower and stem, with a tab on the base of the stem, and then shape the flower in a concave direction. From another print, cut out the bell area on each flower and shape this piece in a convex direction. It will be fixed over the first piece, forming a true bell-shaped flower.

2.   The other flowers in the picture are worked in several layers. To do this, cut out the entire flower and shape them carefully before you glue the layers in place. Finally, cut out a single centre piece or stamens for each flower and fix them in the centre of the flower.

3.   The tree roots will look as though they are emerging from the base print if they are cut out with a tab which can then be inserted through a slit in the base print.

Instructions

You will need six prints to complete this picture if you wish to build up as many layers as shown in the illustrated example. As you proceed, it will be up to you to decide how much you wish to highlight each section. The number of levels you use and the shaping you give each piece will make your work unique. There is no exact method that should be used for a particular piece — simply use the basic techniques in your own way to bring your picture to life.

Work, as usual, from the back of the picture towards the front. Cut and shape a few pieces then glue them into place before moving on to the next area. Remember to colour all white cut edges with a marking pen of the appropriate colour.

1. Use one complete print as the base.
2. Background features. The background features are the flowers, which will be layered to give dimension and which need to be carefully shaped. To do this, take a second print and cut out the flowers behind the mouse and the fairy, with tabs attached. Decide how the leaves and petals should be shaped. Using the shaping tool and mat, shape these pieces so that they have realistic curves. Insert the tabs into the base print and fix them in place with silicone sealer.
3. The bluebells. The first cut-out flower bell should be shaped in a concave direction. Then, cut out a second piece from another print for the front of the flower and shape it in a convex direction, fixing it in place over the first piece. A true bell shape has thus been constructed in these two easy, but very effective steps.
4. The more complex flowers. These are cut in several layers, from the extra prints. Carefully study the flowers, taking note of the layers of petals, stamens and leaves, and work accordingly. You will have to cut through several prints to achieve the layered effect, but remember you have six to work with. Avoid cutting into the fairy and the mouse when working the flowers, as you will need the prints later.
5. The middleground. The middleground features the tree roots, the fairy and the mouse. To achieve the appearance of the tree emerging from the ground, cut a slit through the base print where the roots emerge from the earth. From another print, cut out the tree and roots, with a tab attached to the roots. Shape the tree roots using the tool and mat, and then insert the tabs into the slit in the earth. Thus, you will have a dimensional effect in your picture.
6. When the tree roots have been completed, curve the bottom edge of

the base print forwards and glue a piece of foam core board underneath it for support. This will give the impression of the ground curving up in the front.

7. The mouse. Cut out the mouse in one whole piece, shape it and then glue it in place. Layer the mouse by cutting out separate pieces of its body and clothing, and after careful shaping, glue them in position. Add extra pieces for its coat pocket, the buttons, collar and sleeve.

8. The fairy. The fairy is raised well above the background and her wings and dress are very curved. She, therefore, needs to be supported by something solid, such as a piece of wire or a satay stick cut to the necessary length.

    Cut a complete fairy and work the shaping and curving, then fix her to the satay stick. Work the fairy in layers, cutting out separate pieces for the top layers of her dress, her hair, arms, hands and face. The last layers will be the garland of flowers around her skirt and the bloom in her hair.

    When the fairy has been completed, glue her onto the base print. She needs to be raised well above the base, so you'll need to place a matchbox support under her until the glue dries. Add complete feet with shoes, then an extra layer of shoes fixed on the tree and the ground so they are just visible under her skirt.

9. The foreground. Mushrooms, a gumnut baby and a group of flowers on the right side of the picture are all part of the foreground. Cut out the mushrooms with a tab attached to the bottom edge of the stalks. Slit the base print and insert the mushroom stalks. Also, cut out separate mushroom caps, shape them so they are well rounded, and then glue them on top of the first pieces.

    Layer the gumnut baby in the same way, adding extra pieces for the hair, face, arms and legs.

    Layer the flowers, shaping the petals and leaves before gluing them in place. Cut the lower petals with tabs and sit them under the top petals. Cut extra flower centres and add these to the final layer.

10. Framing. This picture has been framed professionally with a mat board, which has been cut smaller than the picture to allow the mushroom cap and outer flowers to protrude out from the frame.

SWEETPEA BLOSSOM BABY

Artist May Gibbs is famous for her exquisite illustrations of bush babies which adorn the pages of her children's books. This delicately shaded picture of 'Sweetpea Blossom Baby' was worked by Lyn Cunningham who has used a single layer method with carefully shaped pieces to create a pretty three-dimensional tole picture.

STEPS

1.   The technique used for constructing 'Sweetpea Blossom Baby' requires five prints of the picture, which is worked using only one layer of pieces. Many of the pieces are cut out with an extra allowance, which will be hidden under another piece (see, for example, the petals on the lower right-hand side). As a first step, cut out the petals and fix them in place.

2.   As only one layer of prints is used in this example, the shaping of each piece is very important. To give dimension to the finished picture, pieces have been raised well above the background print using blobs of silicone adhesive.

Extra materials

- Spray adhesive.
- Soft lead pencil.

Instructions

1. Prepare the base print by spraying the back of it with spray adhesive. Fix it to a backing board, smoothing out any air bubbles with your fingers.

2. Coat each of the remaining prints with a sealer. Apply one coat and leave it to dry before applying the next. Sealing will prevent oil staining from the silicone adhesive and will also strengthen the paper — which is necessary when cutting out very fine pieces such as the stems.

3. When you have cut all the pieces, colour all the white edges with a soft lead pencil.

4. Outer blossoms. Cut out the outer petals (see Step 1 on p. 30), leaving an allowance on those that will fall behind other petals. This allowance will be covered by the pieces fixed on top, making the flowers appear attached, rather than each one being separate. For example, cut out the bud at top right of the picture in one piece, including the tiny green section at the base of the bud. From another print, cut out the stem with the same green section attached and an allowance on the bottom of the stem. Shape both pieces, and then glue them together, positioning the stem section over the bud piece so that the bud projects from the stem. Glue the new piece onto the base print, placing the stem under the petal (as shown in Step 1 on p. 30). Fix the pieces in place using silicone glue. First glue the pieces which will lie behind others, and then gradually build up the picture by adding those pieces which appear to be on top.

5. Centre blossoms and blossom baby. Cut out the petals closer to the centre of the picture. Continue to assemble pieces as before, referring to the Step 2 picture. Fix the centre flowers then work the blossom baby in separate pieces. Finally, attach the stems and the tiny pieces which sit on top of the flowers.

6. Varnishing. If you wish to varnish the picture, apply a gloss coating, following the instructions given in the 'Basic Techniques' chapter of this book.

BOX WITH PANSIES

Only four cards were used to complete this delightful pansy-topped box. The design on the box was worked by the author, using images from greeting cards which featured a water-colour painting by Celene Ryan entitled *Carol's Rose Garden* (published by Carol Wilson Fine Arts Inc., Oregon). The embossed design on the cards almost eliminated the need for any shaping of the cut-out paper pieces. A timber box, originally made to hold a piece of embroidery in a recessed lid, was sponge-painted in white and gold.

Extra materials

- Wooden box with recessed lid.
- Folk art paint, white and gold.
- Sea sponge.
- Paint palette (or plastic lid).
- Brushes.
- Craft glue.

Instructions

These instructions can be applied to any floral print similar to our pansy design. If the design is not embossed, remember to shape the petals (see p. 11) in a realistic curve before gluing them in place.

1. Use one print to cut out the base design. The flowers and pansy blooms on our box were cut from a greeting card and then re-arranged to suit the box lid. Assemble your paper tole on a cutting mat or cardboard; it will be glued onto the box top when complete.

2. Decide which blooms, or areas of the design, you wish to highlight. Cut out these blooms completely, leaving behind any leaves or stems which you want to appear only on the base print. Dab silicone sealer onto the base print, in the areas you will be highlighting, and place the cut-out blooms onto the sealer. Use the cocktail stick to adjust the angle to suit the blooms. The pansies on our box were pressed in at the centre of each petal, and the edges were lifted a little.

3. Decide which flower petals should stand higher than the rest of the picture. From a third print, cut these petals out, individually, over-cutting any areas which will fall under a following layer. Place dabs of glue onto the main picture. Glue individual petals in place, adjusting their position with a cocktail stick as before.

4. Finally, select the area of the flower you feel should have the most emphasis. We chose to highlight the yellow centres of the two main blooms. From the fourth print, cut out these centre areas, cutting individual petals and following the jagged lines where the colour changes to mauve. Place blobs of silicone sealer in the centre of the flowers on the last layer of the main picture. Position the final pieces (the flower centres), adjusting their angle as before.

5. Prepare the wooden box by painting it with white paint. Leave it to dry thoroughly. Wet the sea sponge and squeeze out excess water.

Dip the sponge into a little gold paint and lightly touch it to the surface of the box without twisting the sponge at all. Repeat until the surface has as much gold paint as you desire. Allow the paint to dry.

6. Use craft glue to fix the paper tole piece to the centre of the lid.

COLUMBINE FLOWER FAIRY

The series of illustrations by Cicely Mary Barker are very popular for paper tole. They have a clear background and a lot of detail with clearly defined outlines. What's more, the subjects of these illustrations are simply enchanting. Our 'Columbine Fairy' was worked by Lyn Cunningham.

Columbine

STEPS

1.　This picture is worked using a layering technique. The first stages of assembly involve building up several layers of the main features of the picture. Each piece must be carefully shaped before it is fixed in place.

Columbine

2.   In the final stages small details are added to enhance the impression of depth. Shoes are added to the feet, top layers of the skirt are attached and top petals and leaves are fixed in place.

Extra materials

•   Spray adhesive.

Instructions

Six prints were used to construct this picture. The technique employed involved layering to build up depth.

1. Spray adhesive to coat the back of one print and adhere it to a backing board. Use the other five prints to build up the layers.

2. Cut out complete pieces of the nymph, the fairy and the plants featured in the foreground. Shape each piece using the sculpting tool and mat. Make sure that you sculpt the wings so that their tips project forward, and the tip of the hat so that it falls backward. Legs, face and body parts should be gently curved.

3. Referring back to the Step 1 picture, fix in place the stem underneath the nymph, and then the nymph pieces. Attach leaves under the fairy's feet, and finally fix the fairy in place.

4. The nymph. Proceed to cut out and layer the nymph in separate pieces for body, legs, arms, sleeves, head, flute and hands. Using blobs of silicone glue, gradually build up the layers, always fixing the pieces which appear to be underneath first. Add separate hat and shoes last.

5. The fairy. Layer the fairy in much the same way as the nymph. First, cut a piece with legs and shoes and fix it in place. Then, cut a complete body including the wings, arms, head and hair. Shape all parts carefully and fix them in place, with the shoes resting on top of the leaves. Next, add a piece which has body, arms and head, but not the flowing hair on top. Then, add separate pieces for the dress and separate pieces for the top layers of the skirt, which appear on each side like petals. Finally, add the hairpiece.

    Refer to Step 2 picture for the following stages.

6. Carefully cut out complete pieces for flowers and stems behind the fairy and the nymph. Fix the flowers and stems in place, positioning the stems over the nymph's wings and behind the fairy's wings. Use a small amount of silicone glue to fix fine stems in place.

7. Build up the flowers by layering the petals and the centres. For the flowers in full bloom, cut a succession of petal pieces, gradually building up to a layer which only has the very top petals. Fix each layer on top of the other, carefully lining up each separate piece.

8. Work the layers on the leafy buds behind the nymph by cutting one or two top leaves and gluing them onto the complete piece.

9. Varnishing. If you wish to glaze the picture, apply a gloss coating, following the instructions given in the 'Basic Techniques' chapter of this book.

ROSE WALL HANGING

A pretty gift is made by mounting this paper tole piece on a wooden plaque with wire hanger, available from craft and folk art suppliers. The roses used for this plaque were cut from a sheet of inexpensive wrapping paper. Only one sheet of paper was required for this plaque as the rose pattern was repeated several times over the paper.

Extra materials

• Painted wooden plaque with wire hanger (available from craft and folk art supply shops).
• Craft glue.

Instructions

1. Select the area, or pattern of the wrapping paper you wish to use for your paper tole, and decide which flower petals you will highlight. Cut out one complete pattern to use for the base print.

2. Cut out multiples of the remaining parts of the design in the following way: first cut large areas with full flowers and leaves. Then, on other prints, gradually reduce the design parts and cut out individual petals, and those sections of the design (flower centres) which you wish to be raised more than others.

3. Curve the cut-out pieces around your fingers. Working on the base print, apply dabs of silicone sealer, then position the full flower and leaf pieces you have cut out. Shape them by lifting them with the cocktail stick and angling them correctly on top of the silicone blobs. One or two full flower pieces could be added to the base print in this way to build up the level of the print. You are then ready to start adding the individually cut-out petals.

4. Add remaining layers to the main piece by dotting small blobs of silicone sealer onto the main work, then adding individual petals or parts of the petal to the piece. Shape and angle the petals as before, using the stick.

5. Finally for the last layers, use only the pieces you want to raise higher than the rest, for example, the flower centres. The petals should be cut out individually and underneath pieces should be overcut (see Chapter 2 on 'Basic Techniques'), so that they can be overlapped. Look at the original print carefully and decide which parts of the design, petals and so on, sit over the other parts. These should be positioned last. Underneath them should sit whole portions of the print which are overcut and include the overlapping part of the design, in order to give a dimensional effect. It sounds confusing, but when you actually start to cut and layer, it will become clear.

6. In the rose design, the centres have been raised above the surrounding petals, and were among the last pieces to be glued in place. When your design is complete, you may wish to give it a heavy coat

of varnish as we did. Apply two or three coats, allowing each to dry before applying the next one. The effect of the varnish on this project was to visually bring the layers together, adding to the overall three dimensional effect.

7. When the varnish is dry, glue the paper tole onto the wooden plaque.

CHRISTMAS DECORATION

Use an illustrated Christmas card to make your decoration which is then mounted on a backing board. Choose a card which has a distinct background and foreground area, and which has clearly outlined features in the illustrations. Because Christmas cards usually change in availability from season to season, these instructions are general rather than specific.

Instructions

1.   Keep one complete card for the base print. Trim it to the desired size and shape.

2.   Use a second card to cut out the entire section you wish to highlight, eliminating unwanted background areas. Cut out pieces of the design you wish to build up from the remaining cards. Shape the cut-out pieces around your fingers echoing the true shape of the elements pictured.

3.   Apply silicone sealer to the base print and build your design in layers, working from back to front. Continue until you have applied the final details to the top layer. In our scene, these were the girl's face, collar and arm.

4.   Apply two or three coats of varnish to your completed paper tole piece. We had the board cut to the desired size by a framer. The piece was then glued in place with the board surrounding it.

5.   Decorate with a ribbon bow if desired.

Information on purchasing the actual prints shown in this book is available from the publisher..

The sheets on the opposite and following pages have been included for you to use in a simple paper tole project.

Cut along the dotted lines to remove the pages from the book.